SEVENTY YEARS

A Platinum Celebration of 'Service Above Self'

COMPILED BY SHARON CHAMBERS

Copyright © 2023 The Rotary Club of Raymond Terrace

All Rights reserved. No part of this publication may be reproduced, distributed, or transmitted in any form or by any means, including photocopying, recording, or other electronic or mechanical methods, without the prior written permission of the Rotary Club of Raymond Terrace, except in the case of brief quotations embodied in critical reviews and certain other non-commercial uses permitted by copyright law. For permission requests, write to the Club Secretary at
sec.rotaryrt@gmail.com

ISBN: 978-0-9946481-7-4

First Edition 2023

M. J. Wright-Editor and Publisher
mjwrightauthor@gmail.com

www.rotaryraymondterrace.com

A catalogue record for this book is available from the National Library of Australia

This summary of 'Seventy Years On ~ A Platinum Celebration of Service Above Self' of the Rotary Club of Raymond Terrace was compiled from three earlier volumes:

'The first 10 years of Friendship, Goodwill, Understanding and Service,

'The First Forty Years'

'Fifty Years of Service' and

'Sixty Years On –
A Diamond Celebration of
Service above Self'

Additional material has been extracted from the Annual Reports from 2013-2023 and from information supplied by members.

TABLE OF CONTENTS

1. FORWARD
2. THE CHARTER MEMBERS
3. HONOUR ROLL
4. SEPTEMBER 1953-JUNE 1964
5. JULY 1964-JUNE 1993
6. TURNING FIFTY AND LOOKING FORWARD
7. THE LAST TEN YEARS
8. ANNIVERSARY MEDIA RELEASES
9. AFTERWORD

FORWARD

The first Rotary Club was formed when Paul P. Harris called together a meeting of three business acquaintances in Chicago USA on 23rd February 1905. It has since grown to a worldwide organisation of 1.2 million people in over 220 countries.

Rotary started in Australia with the chartering of the first Rotary Club in Melbourne in April 1921, spreading to Port Stephens when the Rotary Club of Raymond Terrace was chartered on 8th September 1953.

Bruce McGavin and Max McKenzie, on an approach from the Rotary Club of Maitland, canvassed business, and professional men of Raymond Terrace on the feasibility of forming a local Rotary Club. As a result of their efforts, a meeting of interested and eligible men was held in the top room of the Port Stephens Shire Council Chambers, on the corner of William and Port Stephens Streets. This meeting, attended by Clarry Lawson and Frank Turton of Maitland Rotary Club, resulted in a decision to form the Rotary Club of Raymond Terrace.

Sponsored by the Rotary Club of Maitland, the Rotary Club of Raymond Terrace in subsequent years formed the Rotary Clubs of Nelson Bay, Williamtown, and Raymond Terrace Sunset. Probus Clubs were set up in Raymond Terrace and Medowie.

The concept of Service above self is not unique to Rotary and today we join with many likeminded members and organisations in delivering improvement to the lives of our local, national, and international communities.

On the international stage we have supported the eradication of Polio. Rotary, together with our international partners, are on the threshold of success in fighting this disease.

The Rotary Club of Raymond Terrace has however, always had our local community at the forefront of our planning and action. We have engaged with organisations such as the local schools, the Port Stephens Council, Lions, the Salvation Army, Port Stephens Family and Neighbourhood Services, the Wahroonga Aboriginal Corporation, Men's Shed, Bunnings and other businesses to facilitate significant improvements to the communities of Raymond Terrace and Port Stephens generally. Rotary's leadership has encouraged student skills, community involvement in Australia Day Celebrations, King Street Heritage Festival, other event coordination and assisting welfare providers with necessary resources to benefit the community.

Through Rotary, the Club is well positioned to respond promptly and appropriately to international or local disasters. Clubs in disaster areas can direct 100% of funds and resources received.

'Seventy Years On – A Platinum Celebration of Service Above Self' 1953 - 2023' provides recollections of some of the activities of the Rotary Club of Raymond Terrace that have contributed to the enjoyment and wellbeing of the local community.

Please enjoy a read as we celebrate some of the many ways that Rotary has changed the lives and wellbeing of those around us.

The Charter Members

Fred Anseline
Perc Bettles
Ron Buxton
Les Cave
Jack Cleary (Board Member)
Bruce Donaldson
Ray Elkin
Ben Fuller (Board Member)
Aub Glover
Bob Griffiths
Norm Griffiths (Sergeant at Arms)
Roy Harrington
John Horn
Bruce McGavin (Treasurer)
Max McKenzie (Secretary)
John Monkley
Em Paul
Len Randall (Vice President)
Sam Rodgers (President)
Jim Scott (Board Member)
Lawrie Shearmen (Board Member)
Len Shortland
Roy Wood

Rotary International

NOTICE OF ADMISSION OF THE ROTARY CLUB

OF Raymond Terrace, N.S.W., Australia

Dist. 32   Pop. 4,000

TO:
- OD – 124
- PO
- 330
- 500 – C-62-0
- 600
- 900
- MD
- CEO   See Corr. List No.

DATE ADMITTED: 8 September, 1953

NUMBER OF CHARTER MEMBERS: 23

MEETING DAY: Tuesday

HOUR: 6:15 p.m.

PLACE: R.S.L. Hall

PRESIDENT: Sam Rodgers, Esq.
(Masonite Mfg.)
Glenelg Street
Raymond Terrace, N.S.W.
AUSTRALIA

SECRETARY: Max McKenzie, Esq.
(drapery retailing)
William Street
Raymond Terrace, N.S.W.
AUSTRALIA

DATE ORGANIZED: 21 July, 1953

GOVERNOR: Marshall

SPECIAL REPRESENTATIVE: D. C. Lawson

ASSISTED BY:

SPONSOR CLUB: Maitland

NUMBER OF SUBSCRIPTIONS TO "THE ROTARIAN": **

CORRESPONDENCE— IF NOT IN ENGLISH SHOULD BE IN:

SIGNATURE: HAS

DATE: 8 September, 1953

ROTARY INTERNATIONAL
Chicago 1, Ill., U.S.A., 35 E. Wacker Drive
Zurich, Switzerland, Börsenstrasse 21

APPLICATION For Membership In Rotary International

The Provisional Rotary Club of **RAYMOND TERRACE   N.S.W.   AUSTRALIA**
(State, Province, Etc.)
hereby applies for membership in Rotary International.

This club was duly organized by an authorized representative of Rotary International on **21 - 7 - 1953**
19_____, with **23** charter members, each representing a different business or professional service.

This club hereby declares that it has adopted the Rotary club constitution and that it subscribes to the understandings and agreements printed on pages 2, 3 and 4 of this folder.

The following documents required to complete this application are attached hereto:

1. List of charter members—dated and certified to by signatures of the president and secretary of the club.
2. Check for $100.00 U. S. Currency (or its equivalent)—covering the charter fee as provided in Article 1, Section 2 of the by-laws of Rotary International.

Officers:

Pres. Sam Rodgers
V. P. Norman Griffith
Sec'y Max McKenzie
Treas. Bruce McGavin
S. at A. Len Randall

Complete list of members of the board of directors:

1. Laurie Shearman
2. Jack Cleary
3. Jim Scott
4. Ben Fuller
5. _____
6. _____
7. _____

Regular weekly meetings are held:
Day Tuesday
Hour 6.15 p.m.
Place R.S.L. Hall

Provisional Rotary Club of **RAYMOND TERRACE**

Dated 21st July 19 53
By SAM RODGERS *S. Rodgers*
Club President
Glenelg Street,
~~RAYMOND TERRACE~~
Postal Address

Attest:
MAX McKENZIE
Club Secretary
William St.
RAYMOND TERRACE
Postal Address

LIST OF CHARTER MEMBERS

This list shall contain not less than twenty names nor more than thirty-five, except in cities of more than 100,000, in which case it may contain not more than fifty names.

Forward original and one copy to the District Governor. New club to keep one copy.

THE PROVISIONAL ROTARY CLUB OF Raymond Terrace, NSW, Aust.   List Closed 17 - 7 - 1963

To the Secretary of Rotary International,

The following have been duly elected to and have accepted charter membership in this club and have paid all required fees and dues for the current period.

NOTE: Classification given each member must describe the principal service rendered to the public by his firm.

8409

	1. GEORGE MAXWELL MCKENZIE (18)	5. BRUCE DONALDSON
Name of member		
Club classification	Retail Drapery Retailing	Dental Dentistry (49)
Name of firm	McKENZIES	BRUCE DONALDSON
Executive position	PROPRIETOR	PROPRIETOR
Business address	WILLIAM ST. RAYMOND TERRACE	STEPHENS ST. R. TERRACE
Residence address	22 HARKE ST. HAMILTON N.S.W.	RICHARDSON RD. RAYMOND TERRACE

	2. BRUCE ROBERT McGAVIN	6. WALTER SCOTT
Name of member		
Club classification	Retail Butcher meat retailing	Milk Collection Bulk
Name of firm	BRUCE McGAVIN (28B)	WALTER SCOTT (28-B)
Executive position	PROPRIETOR	PROPRIETOR
Business address	KING ST. RAYMOND TERRACE	HUNTER ST. RAYMOND TERRACE
Residence address	22 ADDISON RD. NEW LAMBTON	HUNTER ST. RAYMOND TERRACE

	3. PERCY CHARLES BETTLES	7. LEONARD GORDON RANDALL (36)
Name of member		
Club classification	(Works) Accountant	Guest Houses Prop.
Name of firm	COURTAULDS (AUST) LTD (14)	SHOAL BAY COUNTRY CLUB
Executive position	ACCOUNTANT	PROPRIETOR
Business address	C/- COURTAULDS (AUST) LTD TOMAGO	SHOAL BAY
Residence address	2 KINDRA EST. RAY TERRACE	SHOAL BAY

	4. FREDERICK ALFRED ANSELINE (20)	8. SAMUEL JOSEPH RODGERS
Name of member		
Club classification	Radio & Electrical equipment Retailing	Works Masonite Mfg
Name of firm	ANSELINES ELECTRICAL SUPPLIES	MASONITE CORPN (15)
Executive position	PROPRIETOR	WORKS MANAGER
Business address	KING ST. RAYMOND TERRACE	WILLIAMTOWN ROAD R. TERRACE
Residence address	KING ST. RAYMOND TERRACE	GLENELG ST. R. TERRACE

(Please indicate which members, if any, were formerly members of a Rotary club, and give name of that club.)

List of Charter Members

The Provisional Rotary Club of Raymond Terrace

Name of member	9. Roy Vincent Hanington (66)	14. John Anton Horn (11)
Club classification	~~Anglican~~ ~~Religion - Christianity~~ Protestantism (Anglican)	Pharmacy
Name of firm	Church of England	Horns Pharmacy
Exec. position	Minister	Proprietor
Bus address	Sturgeon St R. Terrace	William St R. Terrace
Residence address	Sturgeon St Raymond Terrace	Irrawang St Raymond Terrace

Name of member	10. Lawrence Jack Shearman	15. Norman Rees Griffiths (32)
Club classification	Dairy ~~Farmer~~ Farming (3-B)	~~Traffic Officer~~ Public Safety
Name of firm	L. J. Shearman	Police Dept. ~~Police~~
Executive position	Proprietor	Sergeant
Business address	"Portree" Raymond Terrace	William St Ray Terrace
Residence address	"Portree" Raymond Terrace	William St Ray Terrace

Name of member	11. Aubrey Eric Glover (5)	16. Roy Wood (16)
Club classification	Garage & Service Stn.	~~Building~~ Building Construction
Name of firm	Glovers Garage	Roy Wood
Executive position	Proprietor	Proprietor
Business address	Pacific Highway R. Terrace	Wood St Raymond Terrace
Residence address	Pacific Highway R. Terrace	Wood St Raymond Terrace

Name of member	12. John Parker Cleary (Attach to #8)	17. Ronald Buxton (19)
Club classification	~~Engineering~~ Masonite Mfg (70)	Education Secondary ~~School~~
Name of firm	Masonite Corpn. Ltd.	Education Dept.
Exec. position	Chief Engineer	Headmaster
Bus address	Williamtown Rd R. Terrace	Stockton St R. Terrace
Residence address	Warringhi St R. Terrace	Stockton St R. Terrace

Name of member	13. Raymond Bruce Fuller (36)	18. Ernest Paul (46)
Club classification	Hotels	Timber Manufacturing
Name of firm	Junction Inn	Eldon Saw Mills
Executive position	Proprietor	Manager
Business address	William St R. Terrace	Williamtown Road R. Terrace
Residence address	William St R. Terrace	Adelaide St Raymond Terrace

Note: Sign and submit the third sheet of this form in EVERY case.

List of Charter Members

The Provisional Rotary Club of __Raymond Terrace__

19. John Monkley — 32-A
- Club classification: Shire Administration
- Name of firm: Port Stephens Shire Council
- Exec position: Shire Clerk
- Busi address: William St. Raymond Terrace
- Residence address: Irrawang St. Raymond Terrace

additions – per S6

20. Robert Thomas Griffiths — 27
- Club classification: Private Banking
- Name of firm: Bank of New South Wales
- Executive position: Accountant
- Business address: William St, Raymond Terrace
- Residence address: Sturgeon St. "

21. James Spencer Raymond Elkin — 3-B
- Club classification: Livestock ~~marketing~~ / ~~own animal husbandry~~
- Name of firm: Nerco Pty Ltd.
- Executive position: Live Stock Manager
- Business address: Woodlands, Raymond Terrace
- Residence address: "

add to # 3

22. Leslie Cave — 74
- Club classification: Rayon Manufacturing
- Name of firm: Courtaulds (Aust. Ltd.)
- Exec position: Industrial Officer
- Business address: C/o Courtaulds (Aust. Ltd.), Tomago
- Residence address: Kindo Crescent, Raymond Terrace

23. Dr. Leonard Shetland — 49
- Club classification: Physician
- Busi address: Adelaide St.
- Residence address: "

24.

25.

26.

We, the officers of the Provisional Rotary Club of _____ do hereby certify that the above constitutes the charter membership list of this club and that no new members shall be elected until the club has been admitted to membership in Rotary International.

_____ Secretary   _____ President

SEVENTY YEARS OF PRESIDENTS

1953-54 Sam Rodgers
1954-55 Len Randell
1955-56 Bruce McGavin
1956-57 Jim Scott
1957-58 Aub Glover
1958-59 Frank Dunn
1959-60 Frank Edstein
1960-61 Ted Murphy
1961-62 Lou Dechow
1962-63 Bunny Wilkins
1963-64 John Horn
1964-65 Allan Cunningham
1965-66 Fred Anseline
1966-67 Harry Brentnall
1967-68 John Woodbine
1968-69 Ken Cooper
1969-70 Jack Windeyer
1970-71 Arthur Riding
1971-72 Stewart Mordue
1972-73 Charles Buckingham
1973-74 Eric Moxey
1974-75 Don Laverick
1975-76 Kevin Saunderson
1976-77 Ron Statham

1977-78 Don Flynn
1978-79 Merv McLuckie
1979-80 Keith Chauncy
1980-81 Leo McConville
1981-82 Barry Marshall
1982-83 Ron Lovett
1983-84 Fred Preston
1984-85 Ian Matthews
1985-86 Geoff Latona
1986-87 Barry Worley
1987-88 John Beatty
1988-89 Ray Davies
1989-90 Chris Wilson
1990-91 Ken Buckingham
1991-92 Roy Hitchens
1992-93 Howard Grigor
1993-94 Gordon Irving
1994-95 Noel Dippel
1995-96 John Anderson
1996-97 Bill Williams
1997-98 Richard South
1998-99 Ray Beaumont
1999-00 Harold Wood
2000-01 Greg Gannon

2001-02 Steve Frith
2002-03 Laurie Dicker
2003-04 Kerry O'Connor
2004-05 Norm Coventry
2005-06 Steve Frith
2006-07 Peter Spindler
2007-08 Don Wood
2008-09 Richard South
2009-10 Lynne Collins
2010-11 Stephen de Plater
2011-12 Ernie Elbourne
2012-13 John Butcher
2013-14 Noel Frith
2014-15 Ian Matthews
2015-16 Ian Matthews
2016-17 John Chambers
2017-18 Jacky Gendre
2018-19 Steve Merritt
2019-20 Steve Merritt
2020-21 Tracy Jonovski
2021-22 Tracy Jonovski
2022-23 Adam Nicholas
2023-24 Adam Nicholas

MEMBERS PAST AND PRESENT
Rotary Club of Raymond Terrace

Wayne Adnum	Peter Gesling	Stewart Mordue	**Current Members**
John Anderson	Aub Glover	Eric Moxey	
Fred Anseline	David Gordon	Ted Murphy	Osawasu Aiwekhoe
Emma Atkinson	William Gow	Susan Nadfalusi	Ray Beaumont (Hon)
Frank Bardsley	Bob Griffiths	Michael Oakes	William Boyes
John Beatty	Norm Griffiths	Kevin O'Connor	John Butcher (Hon)
Sue Bell	Howard Grigor	Em Paul	John Chambers
Perc Bettles	Hylton Hamilton	Ron Phelps	Sharon Chambers
John Biggs	Roy Harrington	Frederick Preston	Ray Davies
Bob Blackie	John W Harper	Lana Prout	Ernie Elbourne
Harry Brentnall	Warrick Harris	Arthur Riding	Don Flynn (Hon)
Donald Broadbent	Ian Harvey	Len Randall	Noel Frith
Charles Buckingham	Ian Patterson Harvey	Sam Rodgers	Julie Frith (Hon)
Kenneth Buckingham	Roy Hitchens	Stuart Roff	Greg Gannon (Hon)
Malcolm Bull	John Horn	Charles Rowe	Jim Jonovski
Ron Buxton	Gordon Irving	Leeanne Salmon	Tracy Jonovski
Les Cave	Robert Jackson	Michael Salmon	Steve Merritt
Keith Chauncy	Garry Johnson	Kevin Saunderson	Adam Nicholas
Jack Cleary	Stephen Kennedy	Bruce Saywell	Michelle Nicholas
Ken Cooper	Ann Knight	Brian Schuhmacher	Kerry O'Connor (Hon)
Lyn Collins	Bruce Knight	Jim Scott	Ben Robinson
Norman Coventry	John Lamb	Lawrie Shearmen	Richard South
Allan Cunningham	Geoff Latona	Len Shortland	Lee Stanford
Lou Dechow	Don Laverick	Leo Sotiropoulos	Chris Wilson
Ronald Delforce	Michael Leahy	Peter Spindler	
Stephen de Plater	Barbara Lidbury	Ron Statham	
Laurie Dicker	Raymond Longmuir	Kenneth Terry	
Noel Dippel	Ronald George Lovett	Regina Toth	
Bruce Donaldson	Fielding Madden	Thomas Toth	
Brian Douglas	Barry Marshall	Harry Troman	
Jennifer Downey	Louise Marshall	Graeme Valler	
Frank Dunn	Paul Marshall	Johannes Van Haastert	
Frank Edstein	Ian Matthews	Ralph Ward	
Ray Elkin	Ian Robert Matthews	William Williams	
Ron Elliott	Bruce McGavin	Bunny Wilkins	
Roger Englefield	Larry McGrath	Jack Windeyer	
Trevor Etheridge	Max McKenzie	Don Wood	
Steve Frith	Mervyn McLuckie	Harold Wood	
Kevin Frost	Leo McConville	Roy Wood	
Anthony Fry	John Mercer	John Woodbine	
Ben Fuller	Ernest Millington	Barry Worley	
Bruce Gendre	Rory Milne	Chris Yates	
Jacky Gendre	John Monkley		

PAUL HARRIS FELLOWSHIP RECIPIENTS

Past Members		Current Members	
John Beatty	PHF	Ray Beaumont (Hon)	PHF
Sue Bell	PHF+3	John Butcher (Hon)	PHF
Charles Buckingham	PHF	John Chambers	PHF
Kenneth Buckingham	PHF	Sharon Chambers	PHF+3+B
Ken Cooper	PHF+1	Ray Davies	PHF
Beryl Cooper	PHF	Ernie Elbourne	PHF
Laurie Dicker	PHF	Don Flynn (Hon)	PHF
Steve Frith	PHF+1	Noel Frith	PHF
Jacky Gendre	PHF	Julie Frith (Hon)	PHF
Roy Hitchens	PHF	Greg Gannon (Hon)	PHF
Gordon Irving	PHF	Steve Merritt	PHF+6
Goeoff Latona	PHF	Kerry O'Connor (Hon)	PHF+1
Ian Matthews	PHF+1	Richard South	PHF+1
Erika McLuckie	PHF	Lee Stanford	PHF
Mervyn McLuckie	PHF	Chris Wilson	PHF
Frederick Preston	PHF		
Cameron Ramsay	PHF		
Robyn South	PHF		
Jack Windeyer	PHF		
Robert Winder	PHF		
Don Wood	PHF		
Harold Wood	PHF		

Seventy Years

Honorary Members

Ron Swan
Canon Bob Winder
Roy Beatty
John Beatty
Roy Hitchens
Ken Cooper
Don Flynn
John Butcher
Kerry O'Connor
Julie Frith
Ray Beaumont
Greg Gannon

NOTES ON THE YEARS FROM SEPTEMBER 1953 TO JUNE 1964

THE INAUGURAL YEAR

September 1953 – June 1954

Charter President Sam Rodgers

The Club met in the RSL Hall on Tuesday nights. Dinner fees were six shillings and fines were threepence. First Club projects were a very successful Christmas Party for the residents of Oban Nursing Home and a Monster Fundraising Barbecue. Two new members joined, Ken Cooper and Neville Blanche. The inaugural year was very promising and rewarding and established a standard of fellowship that remains an outstanding feature of the Club today.

1954 - 1955   President Len Randall

1955 was 'The Year of the Big Flood'. Two meetings had to be held in the Raymond Terrace Primary School as the RSL Hall was one of several flood refugee centres. About 1500 pounds was raised by the Club for local flood relief. A Monster Barbecue was held at 'Portree', Nelson Plains to raise funds for a town clock.

1955 - 1956   President Bruce McGavin

The year of the Town Clock that was built at a cost of about 1500 pounds. At a meeting held in the Country Club Hotel, Nelson Bay, the members agreed to sponsor a Rotary Club at Nelson Bay. Two Raymond Terrace Rotarians, Past President Len Randall and Neville Blanche agreed to join the new club and assist with its formation.

1956 - 1957   President Jim Scott

President Jim presided at the Charter meeting of the Nelson Bay Club where PP Len Randall was installed as the inaugural President. The local stockyards were repaired and a successful Bushmen's Carnival and Rodeo was held to raise funds to enable work to start on new stockyards. Car trials and a sports carnival were held on Tomago airstrip. The Club initiated naturalisation dinners for new Australians.

1957 - 1958   President Aub Glover

The Club completed building the new stockyards with 'working bees' at night and on weekends. Another Bushmen's Carnival and Rodeo were held. The Club assisted with local fundraising for the Memorial Baths.

1958 - 1959   **President Frank Dunn**

The fundraising continued for the Memorial Baths. Shelter sheds and a barbeque were built at Nine Mile Creek. The Club organised the Raymond Terrace Brass Band and donated funds for instruments. Charter member Fred Anseline was a band member.

1959 - 1960   **President Frank Edstein**

The Club funded and erected a drinking fountain in William Street. A shelter shed was built in Boomerang Park and 400 pounds was donated towards the purchase of a drill hall in Sturgeon Street for use by the Boy Scouts. Playground equipment was provided to St Brigid's School.

1960 1961   **President Ted Murphy**

Funds were raised for the Blind Society by conducting a car trial. Further repairs were made to the shelter shed in Boomerang Park. A naturalisation dinner was held for new Australians and another 'Golden Holden' fundraiser was conducted.

1961 - 1962   **President Lou Dechow**

A 'Golden Holden' raffle was held to raise funds for general community disbursement. The Club funded the 'Molly Cunningham' area of the Raymond Terrace High School Library and repaired the shelter shed at Boomerang Park.

1962 - 1963   **President 'Bunny' Wilkins**

This was a very social year with numerous fellowship functions. Funds were raised and work started on a Memorial Park near the Memorial Baths. New Australians were welcomed at a naturalisation dinner and the First Secretary of the Soviet Embassy visited and addressed the Club.

1963 - 1964   **President John Horn**

President John planned and organised the Rotary Institute (Assembly) that was held at Raymond Terrace High School. An anniversary function was held to celebrate the first ten years of the Rotary Club of Raymond Terrace. The Memorial Park project was completed and the Pre-School Kindergarten was painted. In conjunction with the Rotary Club of Wallsend, a Barnyard Barbeque was held to raise 250 pounds for the Crippled Children's Association. The Club submitted its first nomination for a Rotary Foundation Scholarship and the Japanese Ambassador, Mr Hayashi visited and addressed the Club.

The first 10 years of Rotary at Raymond Terrace saw the Club firmly establish itself. Throughout these formative years funds were disbursed to recognised charities and local schools, youth groups and to the needy and less fortunate.

Meetings continued on Tuesday nights but the venue changed in 1963 to the Spinning Wheel Hotel. Dinner costs rose to seven shillings and fines doubled to sixpence.

THE THIRTY YEARS FROM JULY 1964 TO JUNE 1993

1964 - 1965   **President Allan Cunningham**

Features of this year were a very successful Freedom from Hunger door knock appeal, a Christmas Party for the Oban patients and matching the Club with Liverston-Kingston Rotary Club in the United Sates.

1965 - 1966   **President Fred Anseline**

The main activities undertaken in this year were painting the YMCA hall, a Christmas Party for the Oban patients, a social bowls tournament with the Lions and Junior Chamber of Commerce at the Raymond Terrace Bowling Club and a visit to the Adamstown Rotary Club.

1966 - 1967   **President Harry Brentnall**

This year included painting the interior of the Pensioner's Hall, repairs and renovations to 22 chairs for Oban Nursing Home, work on the Fitzgerald Bridge Park, providing an Air Viva resuscitator for the Fire Brigade, a scholarship for the two senior years at high school and season tickets to the Memorial Pool for Legacy wards.

1967 - 1968   **President Jack Woodbine**

Work continued on the Fitzgerald Bridge Park with the building of a fence, BBQ and swings. Seats were installed in Boomerang Park and the shelter was repaired. A merry-go-round and BBQ were provided at the Water Ski Carnival.

1968 - 1969   **President Ken Cooper**

A Group Study Team visited from Israel and a naturalisation ceremony dinner was held. A Club representative was appointed to the Council Parks and Gardens Committee. The Club participated in the Heart Foundation Doorknock and enjoyed inter-club visits to East Maitland, Nelson Bay, Dungog, Charlestown and Toronto Clubs. Funds were donated to flood relief in India and to high school scholarships.

1969 - 1970   **President Jack Windeyer**

The Club helped with the Freedom from Hunger Doorknock Appeal. A fountain was completed in Rotary Park adjacent to the Memorial Swimming Pool and a time clock was installed at the pool. The first Group Study Team member Bruce Townsend travelled to Israel. A successful White Elephant stall and Bring and Buy Auction was held.

Seventy Years

1970 - 1971 **President Arthur Riding**

The Club hosted a Group Study Team from New Jersey-Delaware. The Club formed a provisional Rotaract Club and two students were nominated to attend the Rotary youth program, Rotary Youth Leadership Awards (RYLA). An emergency telephone number scheme was established.

1971 - 1972 **President Stewart Mordue**

The Rotaract Club was established! The Club visited the Combined Services Clubs at Nelson Bay, Tea Gardens and Dungog. Members also took part in the Freedom from Hunger Doorknock Appeal.

1972 - 1973 **President Charles Buckingham**

An Interact Club was chartered at the high school. Scholarships were awarded to two students to attend high school and an essay competition was held for sixth form students. The Club Contributed to the Fiji Disaster Appeal and a donation was made to the Renal Research Unit. The Club corresponded with the Rotary Club of Goroka, PNG, and two members of a British Group Study Team visited the Club. The Club helped the Senior Citizens Association and beautified Boomerang Park.

1973 - 1974 **President Eric Moxey**

The Club celebrated their 20th anniversary and meetings were moved to Muree Golf Club. An exchange was conducted between the Interact Club and Blakehurst High School. The Club hosted its first Youth Exchange Student, Ralph Allen. Malaysian student scholarships were organised through Pudu Rotary Club in Kuala Lumpur. The Rotary International (RI) President, William C Carter, visited Newcastle and a Group Study Team from Tennessee visited the Club. The Club continued the upkeep of Fitzgerald Bridge Park.

1974 - 1975 **President Don Laverick**

The first International Exchange Student week was held with thirteen students attending. Peter McConville was the first outbound Youth Exchange student to go to Japan. Members were able to assist two families who had their homes destroyed by fire.
Further assistance was given to students in Malaysia.

1975 - 1976 **President Kevin Saunderson**

Rotary signs were erected on the highway entries to Raymond Terrace. Booklets "You and Your World" were provided to high school students. The first Careers night was organised at Raymond Terrace High School and the first short-term student exchange with New Zealand took place. A wine tasting was held at the showgrounds.

1976 - 1977   **President Ron Statham**

A blood pressure testing unit was organised with 750 people attending. The Club enjoyed a Tamboi Queen cruise and theatre visits. An interclub visit was made with Newcastle North Club. The Club sponsored two high school students in Malaysia with school fees and books. Roslyn Taylor and Ross Keating travelled to Germany and Norway respectively on youth exchange. The Club was involved in the Margaret Illukol Project.

1977 - 1978   **President Don Flynn**

The first Art auction was very successful as well as a Melbourne Cup night fundraiser for the Lottie Thorkilgaard Trust. Restoration of the Rotary Clock took place and the Club took out the second prize in the Beer Can Regatta. An interclub visit took place with Charlestown Club. A mobile Blood Pressure Unit was organised. The President's name badges on the collar were updated by the Rotary Annes.

1978 - 1979   **President Merv McLuckie**

The Club celebrated its 25th Anniversary and meetings moved to the Bowling Club. Members were involved in the Clean-up Campaign and Girl Guide Hall extensions. The Club enjoyed a BBQ with the Sydney Rotary Club at Jimmy's Beach and a tour of HMAS Tobruk at Carrington Slipways. 25 Exchange students attended the student week and Brian Gilligan travelled to the USA on Group Study Exchange. Elizabeth Cooper travelled to Belgium and Greg Preston to Germany on Youth Exchange.

1979 - 1980   **President Keith Chauncy**

Wayne O'Connor travelled to the USA on Youth Exchange and Trevor Coles to the UK on Group Study Exchange. A student travelled to New Zealand on the Twin Match Exchange. An Art Auction was held, a Melbourne Cup night for 3H Campaign, as well as a Careers night at the high school and a Youth Exchange Student week.

1980 - 1981   **President Leo McConville**

Participated in the Twin Match Exchange and assisted with work experience and transitional education at the high school. Donated a refrigerator and freezer to Meals on Wheels. The members enjoyed a visit to Nelson Bay Club for their 25th Anniversary. Nelson Bay Rotary was chartered by Raymond Terrace Club. There was an interclub visit from Dungog Rotary.

1981 - 1982   **President Barry Marshall**

There was a large attendance at 'mother club' Maitland's 50th Anniversary. Jack Windeyer became the Club's first Paul Harris Fellow (PHF), and the Rotaract Club celebrated its 10th Anniversary. Nelson Bay Club paid a visit and the members enjoyed reciprocal visits with the newly formed Tenambit-Morpeth Club. Liz Hyde went to Germany on Youth Exchange and a highly successful Melbourne Cup function was held.

1982 - 1983   President Ron Lovett

Attended the William IV Project site and presented a donation. Constructed Irrawang Primary School cricket nets and started building a BBQ in Riverside Park. The Club supported the Twin River Festival with BBQ catering. The Club had good attendance at the District Conference. Sponsored two students for the Youth Exchange Program with Trudy Schumacher going to Canada and Annette Bottrill to Denmark.

1983 - 1984   President Fred Preston

Established a Men's Probus Club in Raymond Terrace and the Club celebrated its 30th Anniversary. The members upgraded Rotary Park at the Memorial Pool, completed the BBQ shelter at Riverside Park and erected fencing at Bettles Park. Supported Raymond Terrace Youth Centre and conducted a Club night at the Coal Loader. Mark Tooth went to USA on Group Study Exchange and Sue Briggs went to Norway on Youth Exchange. Exchange Student week was conducted successfully.

1984 - 1985   President Ian Matthews

Sponsored Rodney Reinhart to Rotary National Summer Science School. Alison Kime went to Japan and Alison Keating to Denmark on Youth Exchange. The Tilligerry Peninsular Probus Club was formed. Barry Worley visited Papua New Guinea on a FAIM Project (Fourth Avenue in Motion, in later years RAWCS – Rotary Australia World Community Service replaced FAIM). Bike Safety Flag Scheme implemented. A Club address, by James Dibble, on the Peer Support Program was well attended. Blue Light Disco started. The Courtesy Award was held, and the Interact Club was reformed. A public address system was donated to Little Athletics. A joint visit with Rutherford-Telarah to Ramsay Fibreglass took place. Ken Cooper was awarded the Club's second PHF.

1985 - 1986   President Geoff Latona

Cricket nets were erected at Irrawang High School. A Rotary versus high school debate was held and a cricket match with the Rotaract Club took place. Signs were provided for the Safety House Scheme. The Courtesy Award was conducted, and the Peer Support Program received continued support. For the first time three candidates were sent to RYLA and Tina Irving went to the USA on Youth Exchange. The International Youth Exchange Week was most successful. A 'Letters for Peace' competition was held. The Club organised the Twin Rivers Fun Run as well as a Charity Golf Day.

1986 - 1987   President Barry Worley

Formed the Raymond Terrace Ladies Probus Club. Started Market Days at Bettles Park using the Lions and Bush Fire Brigade food vans. Set up Irrawang High School's Band room and painted the War Memorial flagpoles. Held a Youth Exchange Student week and Greg Hall went to Germany on Youth Exchange.

1987 - 1988   President John Beatty

The Japanese Consul visited the Club and spoke about the Japanese Culture. The Food Van was designed and built for the Club. A special vintage port bottling took place for the Club. Charity Golf Day was held at Muree Golf Club and a working bee was held at the Botanic Gardens. Polio Plus involvement started and Oz Ski support began. Catered for the Poll Hereford Society Show. Built bus seats and a shelter on the Pacific Highway. Diana Mainprize went to Japan on Youth Exchange and Kerry O'Connor was appointed to the District RYLA Committee.

1988 - 1989   President Ray Davies

The Club's 35th Anniversary celebrations were attended by Dick and Orphalee Smith from our twin club of Bellingham, USA. A club-to-club Youth Exchange with Brad Rose from Bellingham and Alison Wood from Raymond Terrace was arranged. Suzanne Allen travelled to Denmark and Alex Taylor to Netherlands on Youth Exchange. A debate was conducted between Raymond Terrace and Irrawang High Schools. A Group Study Team from District 760 USA visited. A combined meeting with Nelson Bay Club was held at the Rose Farm. A tree planting programme was implemented, and the food van returned a good income for the year.

1989 - 1990   President Chris Wilson

The Club became an incorporated entity. Ken Buckingham went to Papua New Guinea on a FAIM project (in later years Rotary Australia World Community Service replaced FAIM). Funds were spent on the Newcastle earthquake relief and Nyngan flood disaster. Bus shelters were provided and erected at Raymond Terrace High School. Books were donated to schools for Anzac Day. A successful Christmas raffle was conducted in Raymond Terrace Plaza. Tracey Rae left on Youth Exchange to the USA and Citizens Awards were presented to Raymond Terrace and Irrawang High Schools.

1990 - 1991   President Ken Buckingham

There was a dinner and inspection at the Williamtown RAAF Base. The Club sponsored five candidates to RYPEN (Rotary Youth Program of Enrichment), two nominees to RYLA, three students to Science Summer Schools, four placements on New Zealand Twin Match Exchange and Justine Kennedy to Belgium on Youth Exchange. Kerry O'Connor was appointed District RYLA Coordinator. The Club lunched with visiting French Rotarians. President Ken met with Paulo Costa at Taree. Tree planting carried out. Food van catered at Poll Hereford Show, Oz Ski, the Australia Day Breakfast and Stockton foreshore for the Newcastle Regatta.

1991 - 1992   President Roy Hitchens

The Club was awarded the Doug Greenwood Trophy from the District Governor (DG) for the Club's involvement in the Hagahai Project. The Club hosted Eastern Zone Conference. Inauguration of the Pride of Workmanship Awards. Howard Grigor visited the Hagahai Project in PNG and George Anian, FAIM'S PNG Hagahai interpreter visited Raymond Terrace and attended the District Conference. PHFs were awarded to Merv McLuckie, Don Flynn, and Charles Buckingham. Food van catered at Raymond Terrace Australia Day celebrations, Stockton Foreshore for the Newcastle Regatta and Oz Ski. Eleanor Gregory travelled to the Netherlands on

Youth Exchange. Dennis Irving was formally thanked for donation of oil painting that raised $600 for Rotary. Kerry O'Connor was awarded the Governor's Citation for Meritorious Service to RYLA. A Memorial Clock and plaque honouring PP (Past President) and PHF Merv McLuckie were presented to Raymond Terrace Public School.

1992 - 1993   **President Howard Grigor**

The Club achieved a record attendance at the Rotary International Convention in Melbourne. Howard Grigor represented the Club at FAIM (Fourth Avenue in Motion). Food van at Australia Day celebrations, Stockton Foreshore, and Poll Hereford Society Show. Conducted a successful Christmas Raffle. Mounted a plaque of the 'Four Way Test' on the Rotary Clock. Refurbished and updated the speaker's lectern. Pride of Workmanship Awards night successful. Continued commitment to the Blue Light Disco. Justine Titheridge went to Luxemburg and Cressida Strang to Hungary on Youth Exchange.

1993 - 1994   **President Gordon Irving**

The Club celebrated its 40th year of service with emphasis on fellowship. A Birthday Party, Melbourne Cup Dinner, Christmas Party, Australia Day Breakfast in the Park, and a Progressive Dinner were held. The Club hosted a dinner for the Danish Consul and was involved in the Pat Farmer Run local support efforts. Christmas presents were collected and delivered to the Childrens Ward at John Hunter Hospital. Club visits were made to the new Council offices and Irrawang High School. Catered at Stockton for Newcastle Regatta and Oz Ski.

REACHING FORTY YEARS

Past Presidents Ken Cooper and Fred Preston compiled the above year-by-year account of some of the activities of the first 40 years of the Raymond Terrace Rotary Club. They were aware that such a brief compilation necessarily omits much that was both important and enjoyable.

It is presented with the hope that it will serve as a reminder of many happy occasions, worthwhile projects, and personal commitment, and act as a stimulus and inspiration for others to continue community service through the wonderful world of Rotary.

HEADING FOR FIFTY YEARS

1994 - 1995   President Noel Dipple

Sadly, PP and PHF Fred Preston was called to higher service. The Club was involved in a wide variety of activities, including the Junior Poll Hereford Association weekend, moving an aged couple's caravan and annexe from Anna Bay to Raymond Terrace, Oz Ski, and the Twin River Festival. The food van was given a complete refurbishment. PP Howard Grigor was selected to be District Governor (DG) for 1995-1996. Youth Exchange saw Michael Nyssen come from Belgium and Wendy Bowden visited Germany. Mene Hedegaard returned to Denmark and Gabrielle Rumble returned home from Hungary. Two South African Students, Lizl Lamprecht and Joanna Or visited the Club. The New Zealand Twin Match Exchange was successful with Sarah Price from New Zealand and Matthew Burger from Medowie. PP Ken Buckingham let a Group Study Exchange Team to Malaysia. Anthony South attended RYLA, Stacey Thompson and Jock McLauren went to RYPEN, and Marcus Umlaff attended the National Engineering Summer School.

The Club visited Port Stephens Bush Fire Headquarters and presented a donation of $1200 (raised in the previous Rotary year) and enjoyed a visit to Port Stephens Winery. A Christmas Party, a combined meeting with Rutherford-Telarah and a Progressive Dinner were held. The highlight of the year was the 90th Anniversary of Rotary Dinner where PHFs were presented to Ken Buckingham and Beryl Cooper. Kerry O'Connor was awarded a District Governor Citation for outstanding service to RYLA.

1995 - 1996   President John Anderson

The Club was the 'Home of the District Governor', Howard Grigor, who had a memorable year. Eight new members were inducted, one of whom was Emma Atkinson, the first female member of the Club. The 95th Anniversary of Rotary International was celebrated by a special dinner where PPs John Beatty and Gordon Irving were awarded PHFs. Past World President Paulo Costa represented the Rotary International World President Herbert G Brown at the 'Colonial Chann Conference' organised and run by the Club. On his retirement, the NSW Governor, Rear Admiral Peter Sinclair invited the Club President to a Garden Party at Government House.

Our Club and Probus Clubs jointly celebrated the 30th Anniversary of Probus. An auction was held with octogenarian Jack Windeyer helping to raise in excess of $4000. A Christmas raffle was held, and the food van catered at Oz Ski, Newcastle Regatta and Australia Day Breakfast in the Park, Poll Hereford Sale, Medowie Fair and Twin Rivers Festival. About $1400 was raised by a Book Sale and surplus books were given to Belmont North School. Books were also sent to PNG, the Philippines, and Solomon Islands.

Special nights included School Debates, Vocational Awards, Job Talks, worksite visit to Newcastle Airport, a joint meeting at Tenambit-Morpeth, East Maitland Club's Debutante Ball and Ladies Nights. There was a visit by sixteen members to Merriwa, a Car Rally and Picnic, and cruise up the Myall River.

Andrea Zirves visited the Club from Germany and Wendy Bowden returned from Germany. Ben Frost went to Finland and Andrew Deacon visited Argentina. Two students were involved in the NZ short-term exchange. The Club sponsored four candidates to RYPEN one to RYLA and one to Siemens Summer Science School.

1996 - 1997   **President Bill Williams**

Williamtown Rotary Club was chartered on 3rd August 1997 at Fighter World on the RAAF Base. Andrea Zirves returned to Germany. In September the Club catered for 180 young cancer patients from Camp Quality with local businesses providing food and drinks to serve from the Food Van. DG Brian Pattinson visited the Club with dinner at Sir Francis Drake. Past NSW State Governor and Father of the Year, Rear Admiral Peter Sinclair attended the Primary School Debating Competition. The Christmas Raffle was successful and a Christmas Party was held at Zac's at Karuah. PHFs were awarded to Geoff Latona and Harold Wood. Honorary Member Canon Bob Winder was presented with a Rotary Foundation Gift Set of an engraved carafe and glasses. Canon Winder was presented with a PHF at a special Family BBQ commemorating the Call to Higher Service of the Founder of Rotary.

Valeria Rollan arrived on exchange from Argentina and Andrew Deacon and Ben Frost returned from Argentina and Finland respectively. A Charity Golf Day was held at Muree Golf Club raising $2000. At the Dubbo District Conference, the Club was awarded the DG's Special Award for the 'Best Administered Club in the District'. The Annual Awards night was combined with Williamtown Club with the Federal Member for Mackellar and Minister for Defence Industry Science and Personnel, Bronwyn Bishop, addressing the Awardees. A Progressive Dinner was held and worksite visits made to Goldsmith's Frames and Trusses, McLean, Dowding and Mills Electrical Motor Rewinding, and the Australian Defence Industries at Carrington. A combined meeting was held with Newcastle North at the Albion Hotel and the Guides Hall was given extensive renovations and a kitchen refit.

1997 - 1998   **President Richard South**

An eventful year and memorable to all. There were significant changes to membership and the Board. A survey identifying the needs and expectations of Rotary and the Club membership resulted in the formation of the Rotary Club of Raymond Terrace Sunset with Past President Roy Hitchens as the DG's Representative. A significant number of members, including three PPs moved to the new Club. Later, a further eight members, among them five PPs and a Past District Governor left the Club. Despite this reduction of numbers and experience, the Club developed a positiveness that contributed to the successful completion of the set programs and regaining the title of 'The Friendly Club'.

The Club was well represented at District level with PPs Ray Davies and Noel Dipple appointed Assistant Governors (AG), and Harold Wood filled the position of District Treasurer. Brian Douglas and Michael Leahy were formally admitted to the Club. Highlights of the year included: the successful DGs visit with his AG; hosting Valeria and the short term exchange students in our homes and Club; Kylie Petersen's return from South Africa; Past President Ken and Beryl Cooper's start on the long term exchange student history; a successful Christmas Raffle and equally enjoyable and successful Charity Golf Day; the Raymond Terrace/Williamtown joint Vocational Awards Night; awarding a PHF to a surprised Kerry O'Connor and a Four Avenues of

Service Citation to PP Ray Davies; the Primary School debates; the worksite visits to PP Don and Yvonne Flynn's farm and the Westpac Rescue Helicopter. The Club supported almost thirty organisations with donations totalling more than $9000.

1998 - 1999   President Ray Beaumont

Four new members were inducted increasing the membership to 22; this dropped when two members were appointed to Honorary membership. The Australia Day Breakfast and Charity Golf Day were shared with Sunset Club, as was a special dinner where both Clubs gave cheques to the Hunter Medical Research Foundation. PP Roy Hitchens maintained regular visits to Sunset Club in fulfilment of the charter requirements. Harold Wood and PP Ray Davies maintained club representation at District level. The warmth of Club fellowship was a major strength contributed to by our partners and the social occasions of theatre parties, an offshore fishing trip, and our successful challenge to Warners Bay Club for the Staffordshire Pint.
Possession of the 'Pint' was passed to Newcastle Club after they claimed victory at indoor soccer.

Community support and charitable work included: operation of the food van; Christmas Raffle; District car raffle and a Charity Golf Day. Community support was covered by the Pride of Workmanship Awards, Bowelscan and the Australia Day Breakfast. The Club's strong youth support was continued with long-term and short-term youth exchanges, RYLA, RYPEN, RELAYID (Rotary Educational Leadership Award for Youth with Intellectual Disabilities course), Primary School Debates, Summers Schools in Science and Engineering, Camp Quality support, and assistance with literacy development in schools. Several members and their partners visited schools each week to hear children read, and related work.

1999 - 2000   President Harold Wood

During the year four new members were inducted and two resigned to transfer to other Clubs outside the District, bringing the total active membership to 22. Some of the community support and charitable work included the Christmas Raffle, Charity Golf Day, operation and hire of the food van, and the Rotary Debutante Ball. Other activities were the Trade Scholarship Award, Pride of Workmanship Awards, Bowelscan, Australia Day celebrations, and grocery packing for the Raymond Terrace Neighbourhood Centre. The Club continued its support for youth with the Youth Exchange Programs, RYPEN, Siemens Summer Science School, assistance with literacy development in schools, support of Camp Quality, the Primary School Debating Competition, and the presentation of books to the high schools for ANZAC Day. Richard Finlay-Jones was sponsored to visit Norway on a Group Study Exchange.

2000 - 2001   President Greg Gannon

Interaction with other Rotary and Service Clubs was extensive throughout this year. Working with Raymond Terrace Lions to staff the Holden BBQs and cater for the local section of the Olympic Torch Relay was successful both for the Club and community. The President represented the Club at Kiwanis and Men's Probus Changeovers, Ladies Probus Christmas Luncheon, Lions Combined Services Night, and the Air Force Week Cocktail Party. A later highlight of the year was the combined meeting with Sunset and Nelson Bay Clubs. Four members and partners attended the District Conference in Maitland.

On Youth Exchange. Cate South left for Denmark and Corentine Le Saint arrived from France. The Club hosted a Group Study Exchange team from Finland, and sponsored applicants to RYLA, RYPEN, RELAYID and Summer Science Forums. A Primary School Debating competition was held and books were presented to the high schools at ANZAC Day services.

Discussions were held with Port Stephens Council on selecting a site for a proposed rotunda to celebrate the Club's 50th anniversary. Funding for the rotunda was boosted by the theatre night in Sydney with 50 Rotarians, partners and friends attending 'Shout'. Other events included extensive use of the Food Van, Christmas Raffle and District Car Raffle. The Charity Golf Day was a great success with proceeds donated to the Hunter Medical Research Institute. Community support activities included the Trade Scholarship Awards, Pride of Workmanship Awards, Community Awards, Bowelscan, Australia Day Celebrations and the grocery packing for the Raymond Terrace Neighbourhood Centre.

Membership remained steady with two inductions and one resignation and the call to higher service of Charter Member and PHF, PP Bruce McGavin. The partners group continued their support program with monthly meetings and a Progressive Dinner.

2001 - 2002   President Steve Frith

Youth projects included the Primary School Debates, the Summer Science School at Canberra, ANZAC Day book presentations to the High Schools, RELAYID, Siemens Summer Science Forum, and the Drive Alive course. Community support was achieved by use of the Food Van, Christmas Raffle, Charity Golf Day, Bowelscan, and the Australia Day celebrations.

Throughout the year there was a diverse and extensive range of guest speakers who kept members interested and entertained. This was supplemented by the International Service toasts to overseas clubs. Cate South returned from Denmark and the Club co-hosted Julie Neilsen from Denmark with Adamstown Rotary Club. Pride of Workmanship Awards and the Encouragement Award were presented at a special dinner by Bob Horne. Members were saddened by the passing of Honorary Member, PP and PHF Charles Buckingham.

The first non-progressive dinner was held at the Boat Club at Grahamstown. Three members attended the District Conference at Forster.

2002 - 2003   President Laurie Dicker

The year started with a visit to the Club by DG Alf Braye and AG Peter Thraves, accompanied by their partners. Community events attended included Lions and Probus Changeovers, The Airforce Week Cocktail Party, and a Sponsors Lunch at the Hunter Botanic Gardens. District Presidents Meetings were informative and provided an opportunity to meet other Presidents.

Three members resigned due to business and work commitments, but the Club stayed strong and committed. Interesting guest speakers from industry and community organisations provided entertainment. The Federal Member for Paterson Bob Baldwin spoke on the Year of the Outback and the members and their partners were introduced to the elements of Tai Chi. Public Liability insurance became a focal point and John Bartlett MP addressed the Club on new legislation introduced to restrict the surfeit of public liability claims. The Club visited Hunter Wetlands, the Karuah By-pass, and the Rutherford/Telarah Rotary Club.

Involvement in the long term Youth Exchange Program continued with Alexander Montgomery leaving for Norway and Ayumi Okamura arriving from Japan. Support for youth was given in the RYLA, RYPEN and RELAYID seminars. Brooke Perkins attended the National Summer Science School in Canberra. Club members assisted in running the Newcastle Science and Engineering Challenge for Year 10 students state wide.

The Rotunda Project was started and other projects during the year were Pride of Workmanship Awards, Trade Scholarship Awards, Adopt-a-Road, Primary School Debates, catering for Camp Quality, Australia Day Breakfast, Kid's Big Day Out, Christmas Raffle and Bowelscan. Kerry O'Connor was appointed to convene at the combined Probus Club of Medowie.

TURNING FIFTY AND LOOKING FORWARD

2003 - 2004   President Kerry O'Connor

Members celebrated the Club's 50th Anniversary with a Birthday Dinner and presentation to the community of a Rotunda donated by the Club and located in the Hunter Botanic Gardens. The first member to be inducted after the Club was Chartered, PP and PHF, Ken Cooper, had his fifty years of service recognised by Rotary International.

A combined Probus Club was founded in Medowie with over 70 Charter members. Our Club membership remained at 20 with the transfer of one member to the newly formed Club of Myall Shores and the induction of a former Rotarian from New Zealand.

The Club supported District events and projects as well as Pride of Workmanship, Bowelscan, Adopt a Road Campaign, Australia Day Celebrations and Learning for Life. Youth activities were strongly supported with the Primary School Debating Competition and involvement in the Newcastle Science and Engineering Challenge as well as RYPEN and RYLA. Books were presented to the two high schools to commemorate ANZAC Day. Over $25,000, which included the cost of the Rotunda, was donated to these and other community organisations.

There was a strong emphasis on fellowship and the family, with greater involvement in activities organised by partners. Among these were a Movie Night, Picnic and Games Day, an Introduction to New Products, Dessert and Port Night, Macadamia Nut Farm Products, and a Pot Luck Supper. Members and Partners visited the local Mushroom Farm and the Ten Pin Bowling Centre. At the 2004-2005 Changeover, PP and PHF, Ken Cooper was appointed by the Club to be the first Honorary Life Member.

2004 - 2005   President Norm Coventry

Our objectives to re-introduce a Rotaract Club and the formation of a PCYC Club were too ambitious to achieve in one year, however the seeds were sown. Discussions and visits to our Club by local police were encouraging.

Our focus of increasing membership saw the induction of Bob Blackie, David Gordon, and Peter Spindler, however, John Mercer resigned, resulting in 22 members.

Together with the Rotary Club of Williamtown, we celebrated the 100th Anniversary of Rotary at a dinner with 34 Rotarians and 44 guests. Guest speakers, Ken and Meryl Williams, spoke about their experiences in Africa. A tribute to seventeen PHFs was a fitting way to recognise our community contribution to Service Above Self in our centenary year.

We enjoyed a visit to the Belmont Club, the first visit in over thirty years, and took the opportunity to exchange ideas.

DG, Michael McNamara and his wife Helen visited during October. The DG expressed that our Club was one of the most welcoming that he had been to, reinforcing our motto as the 'Friendly Club'.

Fundraising focused on the food van and the annual Christmas Raffle. Our community involvement included Bowelscan, Adopt a Road clean up and Australia Day catering. Youth remains a priority with participation in the annual primary School Debating, sponsorship of a student within the Smith Family program, sponsorship of students to RYPEN and the National Youth Science Program. This year there were no international exchange students.
Guest speakers were frequent varied, and interesting.

2005 - 2006   President Steve Frith

President Steve was the first Rotarian in the history of the Club to be President twice.

Youth Service – supported the debating competition between the eight Primary schools. The quality of the debating was very high with the final debate won by Medowie Public School. The Club presented books to both high schools for ANZAC Day. Community Service – The Club farewelled the van after many years of faithful service, with the crewing and towing of the van taking its toll. We held the Christmas Raffle and participated in Bowelscan. Club Service – A variety of speakers covered many subjected. Vocational Service – An excellent Pride of Workmanship Awards was held.

Unfortunately, at the start of the year we lost several members due to outside pressures. Our biggest challenge remained to recruit some younger members to ensure the Club's future. The Rotary Annes ran several events during the year, the most outstanding being the Christmas in July.

2006 - 2007   President Peter Spindler

A very active year with supporting local youth and adults in several ways, sponsoring many to weekends away at a variety of youth programs, overseas exchange programs and Group Study

Exchange programs as well as overseas Rotary events. Involvement continued in community events such as the Dragon Boat races, Newcastle Bike Ride, Australia Day, Adopt-a-Road and Clean up Australia.

Once again, our Primary School Debate was successful and the Pride of Workmanship Awardees showed the calibre of employees that are in businesses around the town.

The Club supported the Try-A-Trade event at the Aquatic Club in combination with other local Rotary Clubs. We part sponsored Laurie Kerr to Vanuatu for the Rotary Sew-Aid project. This enabled members to see how Rotary is working in communities overseas that do not have the services and facilities we are used to in our society.

Taking over the Interact Club of Irrawang High School at the start of the Rotary year presented challenges as the Interact Club was endeavouring to gain enough new members to charter. The paperwork was lodged and it had a full representation of board members for the next year with several community events locked in. It was hoped the Club would continue in strength.

Several prospective new members showed interest in joining the Club. On a sad note, Erica McLuckie, and Reverend Bob Winder, both PHFs, passed away during the year. They will be remembered for their service to the Club.

2007 - 2008   President Don Wood

'Rotary Shares' – the Rotary International Theme for the year 2007-2008. Don Wood was thankful to the members for the opportunity and privilege of serving as the President.

Four new members were inducted: John Butcher (Merle) - Communications; Stephen de Plater (Janine) - Religion; Jennifer Downey – Education and Noel Frith (Cherilyn) – Education.

John Beatty was granted an Honorary Membership and Steve Frith was awarded a PHF.

The major fundraising projects were successful – the Christmas Raffle survived the vandalism, the Garage Sale, and the Sausage Sizzle at Bunning.

The Club held many social events: several Ladies nights, Christmas in July at the Friths, Fun, Food and Fellowship at the Souths, Melbourne Cup Races at Muree, Club Christmas Party at Sir Francis Drake Hotel, Sherry and Christmas Cake at the Wood house, New Years BBQ at the O'Connor's, and inter-club visit from Myall Shores Rotary Club.

2008 - 2009   President Richard South

While not really embracing this year's theme of 'Make Dreams Real' we continued our involvement with the community through our Youth Programs, Vocational recognition, and community activities.

There have been changes and challenges along the way with no Christmas Raffle, reduced membership, demands on our time available to provide services and with catering numbers required for each Monday's meetings.

Donations were made to Public Schools Debating, other schools, Pride of Workmanship Awards, Smith Family – Learning for Life, the Rotary Foundation, Australian Rotary Health Research Fund, RELAYID, Youth Exchange Program and RYLA.

A surprise donation from the previous Meals on Wheels allowed us to assist Port Stephens Home Modification Services with the purchase of four items of equipment to assist their clients.

The District Meetings format changed under DG Alex McHarg, with the sessions becoming information sessions focused on problems and directions for clubs as well as the District. This continued at the Health and Harmony Conference in Forster where we had an excellent representation. We could see firsthand how Rotary makes a difference in so many ways and gave us the opportunity to relax together and socialise with old and new friends.

2009 - 2010   President Lynne Collins

RI President John Kenny encouraged us with his inspirational theme 'The Future of Rotary is in YOUR hands'. Throughout the year we witnessed this as various members contributed to the overall running and functioning of our Rotary Club. Our members made a difference to the community and to our Club.

Throughout the year we raised money and gave some financial assistance. At the close of the year, we donated to three charities within the Hunter area: Hunter Melanoma, Prostate Cancer Research, and the Rotary Foundation.

Interesting guest speakers and site visits occurred during the year. We farewelled Harold and Joan Wood who moved to Victoria and welcomed Kellie Mann as a new member.

Throughout the year the Rotary Annes provided much appreciated help and assistance with our clean-up days and community sausage sizzles.

2010 - 2011   President Stephen de Plater

The Rotary International theme was 'Building Communities, Bridging Continents'. As the year progressed, Rotary the world over was called upon to live up to that theme, and in our Club we carried our share of that responsibility. Natural disasters around the world saw the Club punch above its weight with the provision of three Shelter Boxes.

We sponsored one participant in the National Youth Science Forum, two participants in a Science Experience in Sydney, supported Jade Seymour when she attended the NASA Engineering School in the USA and supervised Bowelscan in Raymond Terrace.
The Annual Primary Schools Debating competition lived up to the standards set over previous years. Another highlight was the Vocational Services Award night where Pride of Workmanship was celebrated in our community with a record number of awardees and gave us the opportunity to showcase Rotary.

The work with 'Youthies' should be a vital part of our interaction with the community of Raymond Terrace. As an ongoing event it would demand an extra level of commitment. It would be one of those special things that this Club would be remembered for when histories are written.

The trip to Mary Poppins, despite the confusion by the booking office in Sydney, not by the Club, was a resounding success.

2011 - 2012   President Ernie Elbourne

The 2011-2012 Rotary year was an exciting period with many new initiatives commenced and achieved. Achievements included:

- The erection of promotional signs on main roads into the township, displaying the Rotary Wheel, a symbol of the Club's presence in Raymond Terrace.
- Purchased two pull up banners for display at community events.
- Acquisition of a new BBQ food trailer, that is the envy of other Service Club organisations.
- Successful Christmas Raffle.
- Expansion of the catering services to include Bunnings Maitland, Bunnings Taylors Beach, and Masters Rutherford. We continued to operate our successful BBQ on Australia Day. Our success in these ventures was a credit to all those members who gave willingly of their time and effort in the organisation and operation of these venues. We lived up to the 'The Friendly Club' and the fellowship and enjoyment was reflected in the level of engagement of the members.
- Promotion of Macular Degeneration Awareness Week in Raymond Terrace Marketplace.
- New Generation programs continued to be our strength.
- Supported the two high schools through their Annual Presentation Evenings and the eight primary schools with the very successful Debating competition.
- RYPEN, supported five nominees and sent three from our Club.
- RYLA, with one candidate sponsored by the Club.
- NYSF, we co-ordinated sending an excellent student from our area.
- Bowelscan in the community.
- Vocational Awards Night, where five nominees from employers in the Raymond Terrace District were recognised.
- Interesting and informative guest speakers as well as a site visit to the Raymond Terrace Police Station.
- Welcomed new member Ian Matthews (Sue) to the Club.

The successful year allowed the Club to particularly support local community organisation and the Hunter Health Research with donations to Port Stephens Disability Services, Hunter Prostate Cancer Centre, Hunter Breast Cancer Foundation, Rotary Foundation and Australian Rotary Health. We certainly embraced the Rotary Theme – 'Reach Within to Embrace Humanity'.

2012 - 2013   President John Butcher

The Club established five working committees. This structure allowed a focus on the relevant activity while providing a wider involvement for all members. The primary focus was to increase the membership, support the needs of local schools and raise community awareness of Rotary.

Main sources of funds were derived from 'sausage sizzles' at various local sites and a Christmas Raffle held in the local shopping mall. It was noted that many of the public were aware of the work of Rotary and often donated without wanting to participate in the raffle. Expressions such as 'we know Rotary does good in the community' were heard.

We hosted Taylor Cyopick, an exchange student from St Catherines in Canada. Taylor gained broader experience through the Club activities and the Club gained an increased knowledge of Canada.

Sadly, Roy Hitchens, the oldest member in the Club passed away in March 2013. Roy joined the Club in 1981 and was President in 1991-1992.

The Club appreciated the presence and support of partners at many of the meetings and particularly when hosting visitors. The ladies had their own meetings each month at an adjacent local venue.

Throughout its history the Rotary Club of Raymond Terrace has supported District 9670 with many active Directors and representatives on committees as well as PP Howard Grigor being a District Governor.

THE LAST TEN YEARS OF THE ROTARY CLUB OF RAYMOND TERRACE TO 2023

2013 – 2014   President Noel Frith

Rotary International Theme - Engage Rotary Change Lives

- Youth Programs: RYPEN, students gifted and talented programs, Science and Engineering Challenge, Primary School Debates, National Youth Science.
- 60th Anniversary with 70 attending a special dinner raising $2300 to support the new Health One offices.
- Ken Cooper was honoured with a sapphire Paul Harris pin, and along with Beryl cut the anniversary cake. Don Flynn was made an Honorary member.
- Pride of Workmanship Awards recognised several individuals as well as two teams from Port Stephens Council.
- Port Stephens Family and Neighbourhood Services was assisted with equipment to their new 'Deck' and the provision of food from our BBQ.

- Fellowship through fund raising BBQ's, guest speakers included the GSE team, Jacky Gendre on her roll in Africa and a site visit to Varley Engineering.
- International Exchange saw Taylor Cyopick, from Canada, join us for 6 months together with Lana Prout and the de Platter's hosting her.

2014 – 2015   President Ian Matthews

Rotary International Theme - Light up Rotary

- Primary School Debates were the corner stone of this year's Youth services along with continued support for the 'Deck'.
- We achieved a balance between BBQ fundraisers, including the Matara Hill Climb, and providing services to the community.
- Fellowship thrived with these outings, guest speakers and interclub visits. There were four site visits, including two to Health One.
- Health One received the benefits and more of last year's 60th Anniversary Dinner with a Patient Lift Hoist and Picture Hanging System.
- 'The Screed' was a joint winner along with Williamtown's 'Hornet' for the Jim Henderson District Award.
- We also won the Districts Harold Chadwick Attendance Award for the highest percentage of members partners attending the District Conference in Forster.
- International fundraisers, with two movies, supporting Shelter Box and Polio Plus. Jacky continued her work with RAWCS Lotumbe Community Development.
- Ray Davies had a radio slot with Port Stephens FM while the club also supported King St Heritage Festival and Light up Newcastle – Chinese New Year.
- Pride of Workmanship Awards recognised several individuals and Wing Commander Peter Cluff spoke on the re-development for the Joint Strike Fighter.

2015 – 2016   President Ian Matthews

Rotary International Theme - Be a Gift to the World

- The BBQ was the centre of fundraising, along with Bunnings, Matara and the total organisation and running of Australia Day Markets and Entertainment for the Council.
- Primary School Debating and the 'Deck' again were the highlight of our youth programs.
- John Butcher had a difficult task of following Stephen de Platter with the Screed but ensured everyone was up to date on past and future events.
- The Mudgee District conference was well attended by the Club.
- Once again we supported King St Heritage Festival and Light up Newcastle – Chinese New Year. Utilising, for the first time, our Traffic Control registration.
- Always known as the friendly club, we continued to have entertaining site visits and guest speakers. Mike Rabbitt of NBN spoke and presented the Pride of Workmanship Awards.
- Jacky continued her work with RAWCS Lotumbe Community Development as part of our international outreach.

- Our profile in the community was enhanced by Ray's Radio talks with other interactions by John Chambers and Jacky Gendre in the local community.

2016 – 2017   President John Chambers

Rotary International Theme - Rotary Serving Humanity

- Under John's stewardship and the network developed by Raymond Terrace Rotary there was a significant involvement in the following community programs: -
    - Indigenous Bike and Fitness Track and Sensory Space for Children at Raymond Terrace Primary School. The project supported the Smith family's at risk preschool students and a useful resource for the primary students. The construction consisted of a dry creek bed, a smoking ceremony site, cubby house, humpies, tepees, didgeridoo balance beams, boomerang seats and a garden setting for a yarning circle. Rotary was complimented by Hunter River High teachers and students, Nyugumba Men's group, Wahroonga Aboriginal Corporation and the Raymond Terrace Men's Shed. The outdoor setting was donated by Home World Heatherbrae.
    - Involvement with White Ribbon Day / Got Your Back Sista also involve Wahroonga, Worimi and Hunter River High. This was followed by involvement with a Domestic Violence Refuge in conjunction with Port Stephens Family and Neighbourhood Services, Council, Police and other volunteer trades.
    - Partnering with Red Eye Café, Anglican Church and other community groups Rotary assisted with 'Milo's Table' where a free meal was provided to the homeless, needy, lonely and others just wanting some company to talk to.
    - At a meeting with Wahroonga Aboriginal Corporation, R T Family Practice, Health One and Rotary, arrangements were put into place to facilitate disadvantaged and Indigenous people to a consulting room where these patients could receive help in completing forms or, advice and services, often with the benefit of bulk billing. One program introduced was the Black Dog Program. Privacy and sensitivity provided a win-win for all concerned.
    - A Driver Training Program was established in order that young people, mainly from low socioeconomic backgrounds, who didn't have access to a vehicle or the necessary driver trainers, could gain their licence. The program was financed by the Port Stephens Local Area Command and Raymond Terrace Rotary with a vehicle supplied by Klosters Raymond Terrace and other community groups and the Council's Road Safety and Traffic Officer. Many factors had to be addressed to ensure that all risk management, insurance and training of 'Mentor' driver trainers were covered, along with the young participants. Media covered the opening and members of Parliament, and the police magazine covered its operation.
- Australia Day Markets and Entertainment were continued under Rotary's organisation.
- We had District representation again with Jacky Gendre on the Foundation Committee. Other clubs received Jacky's assistance ensuring grants fully utilised all the funds available and our Club received support as well.

- We catered for the SES training weekend held over three days at Glenbawn Dam. We managed to feed the hungry crews even when they kept on lining up for more. They want us to cater for future events.
- Pride of Workmanship Awards were well supported by businesses and service providers. We started recognising services with two senior officers from the Port Stephens Area Command. White Ribbon Chairman, Jon Chin, was the guest speaker and during the night he presented a cheque to Port Stephens Family and Neighbourhood Services for their new refuge.
These funds were part of the funds raised at the White Ribbon Day.
- Youth areas mentioned above as well as the primary school debates, remained a priority for the Club.

2017 – 2018   President Jacky Gendre

Rotary International Theme - Make a Difference

- Fundraising efforts continued with Bunning at Heatherbrae in place of Taylors Beach along with Tocal Heritage Day parking, Trivia night, Christmas Raffle, and the King Street Festival.
- Youth programs progressed, with Debating, and the Driver Training continued to be developed and controlled with some police volunteering to train participants as well as a new initiative for a school literacy program.
- Working with the Salvation Army, Rotary and Lions installed a shower on their premises for the homeless and arranged for Bunnings to supply secure storage lockers.
- Pride of Workmanship Awards were well supported by businesses and service providers. NSW Fire and Rescue along with the Wahroonga Aboriginal Corporation service providers were recognised.

2018 – 2019   President Steve Merritt

Rotary International Theme - Be an Inspiration

- Meetings were still on Monday nights, however we moved to the Bowling Club.
- The Club continued to support the Salvation Army, Wahroonga, and Friends with Dignity with Rotary programs. This was augmented by the ability to receive and redistribute 90 bed ensembles. This started, what is now known as our Furniture Bank Program, where donated household items have been repurposed to the needy. PP Ken Buckingham allowed us to install a 40-foot container to store items before they are supplied through referrals from local agencies.
- Australia Day organisation continued to provide a wonderful celebration for all the community and involved indigenous organisations in Raymond Terrace and Port Stephens.
- Bunnings, Christmas raffle, Trivia night and traffic control all contributed to enable the Club to serve the community.

- With commitments increasing we have ensured members are updated by the Screed and an understanding that members 'come when you can, do what you can' emphasis. There was an increase on calling on Friends of Rotary.
- Primary School Debating, Pride of Workmanship Awards, suppling meat products to the needy donated by Terrace Meats continued to be well received. Lions Driver reviver was supported by some of our members.
- Rotary 'People of Action' signs replaced our aging public signage along with Internet and Facebook images.

2019 – 2020   President Steve Merritt

Rotary International Theme - Rotary Connects the World

- PP Steve Frith was suddenly called to 'higher order' early in 2020, an exceptional member whose tireless efforts will be missed forever.
- Furniture Bank activities continued to grow exponentially, including support for areas outside of Port Stephens, while new programs of School Back Packs and a Toy Drive were welcomed by the community. Tracy Iles, the Salvation Army captain, opened plenty of doors to assist the community, but sadly she was transferred to Toronto just before Christmas.
- Prior to the Christmas Raffle we extended ourselves and undertook six catering events over four weeks. After Australia Day, events dried up due to COVID-19.
- Port Stephens Family and Neighbourhood Services received funds to enable a 'I Respect' program at the Raymond High School to raise awareness around domestic violence concerns. The Club applied for a grant to further this program to 'Train the Trainer' education for their facilitators.
- A Federal Grant was made to purchase a new Furniture Bank trailer.
- In addition to the Clubs contribution to local needs, we assisted in raising funds for 'Maddies Wish', donations to Backpack and Toy Drives as well as meat supplied by Terrace Meats to the needy. The Furniture Bank contributions were immeasurable.

2020 – 2021   President Tracy Jonovski

Rotary International Theme - Rotary Opens Opportunities

- COVID-19 ensured that we needed to engage in using different platforms and ideas to still be relevant in the community.
- Face masks provided a new source for fundraising.
- No Christmas Raffle resulted in a Toy Appeal with distribution through the Salvation Army.
- The Backpack program more than doubled with the assistance of 60 fully stocked bags from Friends With Dignity.
- We once again embraced an opportunity to assist with the organisation of the King St Heritage Festival. With former assistant organiser Adam Nicholas as one of our members,

- we endeavoured to make the event one for the whole community, like Australia Day, including arranging for the William the IV to return to Raymond Terrace.
- Bunnings restarted at the end of the year with restrictions, and we started using 'square' for cashless payments for the first time.
- No School Debate or Pride of Workmanship Awards took place this year. A restricted Australia Day occurred at Lakeside Leisure Centre.

2021 – 2022   **President Tracy Jonovski**

Rotary International Theme - Serve to Change Lives

- Australia Day celebrations this year returned to normal with Adam's careful management of the event ensuring success. The same result for the King Street Festival in difficult circumstances due to wet weather resulting in 'plan B' organised with Terrace Central.
- The Toy Drive was a huge success with Grandparents As Parents Support Group along with Port Stephens Family and Neighbourhood Services being very grateful for all the donations.
- Backpacks were again distributed together with a new program of providing ladies hygiene products in the form of dignity support packs.
- Lismore flood relief saw the BBQ used to raise funds while a donation of new clothing was distributed locally to relevant charities.
- The Furniture Bank was still in great demand. A Council grant was received to refurbish the BBQ trailer. A refiguration took place where we could lift off the BBQ and use that trailer for the Furniture Bank. We arranged with Council to utilise an unused site at Lakeside. PP Steve Merritt obtained a Federal Government Grant to acquire two new storage containers that were installed in 2022-2023.
- Arrangements were made with the Rotary Club of Terrigal to purchase Shelter Sleeping Bags to supply to local charities with homeless programs.
- Surplus wool supplies were donated to local knitters who made rugs for the needy in our community.

2022 – 2023   **President Adam Nicholas**

Rotary International Theme - Imagine Rotary

- Furniture Bank has installed two containers in Lakeside with a side access installed in one to enable Rotary's many assets to be store securely in one place. A dividing wall will be installed.
- Ray Beaumont and Greg Gannon recognised as Honorary members.
- Primary School Debates continued with the final held at Scotties Cinemas. Irrawang and Grahamstown Public Schools received funds for School Literacy.
- Our BBQ had quite a workout during the year, including new events from Touch Football at Mallabula to Legacy Markets at Nelson Bay to Triathlon at Anna Bay and finally at Raymond Terrace for the Bike leg of another triathlon. These events are as much about fellowship as they are to provide a satisfying meal to the gatherings.

- The Christmas raffle was well supported in both Raymond Terrace shopping centres as was a community Christmas Event at Terrace Central where $1000 was raised for the State Emergency Services.
- Rivergum Grandparents As Parents Support Group received the remaining Backpacks that were put together at a Club meeting. Adam provided the group with training on their square point of sale system.
- Australia Day, organised for the Port Stephens Council, was a great example of how we network with everyone to provide a fun, relaxing and well supported Community event. We were well aided by Friends of Rotary and all Club members.
- The Screed was again recognised for its high standard and content to keep all members and the District updated on our activities. We have commenced consolidating all our Club records / history in one secure location. This will be very beneficial for the upcoming 70th Anniversary and the years to come.

Media Releases for the 70th Anniversary

AUSTRALIA DAY

One of the enduring connections between Rotary and the local community is the Australia Day Celebrations at Riverside Park, Raymond Terrace. For the past 25 years Rotary in conjunction with the Lions has been part of this Council funded celebration. Over the years Rotary's role has increased to the point where, under the guidance of Steve Frith, Rotary became the event organizer of everything from traffic control to entertainment and the delivery of the Community Big Breakfast sponsored by the Raymond Terrace Bowling Club.

Little does the community know the amount of compliance paperwork and organization that goes on behind the scenes to deliver everything from the timing of the Citizenship Day ceremony to speed boat racing, street closures and the various forms of entertainment, planning for which covers several months in the lead up to the event.

Australia Day Raymond Terrace is truly a family affair that each year kicks off with a Free Big Breakfast served by the combined resources of Rotary and the Lions and funded by the Raymond Terrace Bowling Club. The free bacon and egg sandwich or sausage sizzle, free fruit and drinks make a great way to start to a daylong carnival punctuated by a Citizenship ceremony and RAAF fly by.

With the perfect play on words, Rotary can joke that we do the "Lion's share of the work on Australia Day" when in fact, Australia Day is just one of many situations when our community organizations come together to deliver for our community. This teamwork between the likes of the Lions, the Salvation Army, Council, the Men's Shed and the Bowling club is a feature of the way in which our club continues to help deliver for the community in so many different areas.

Today the work of Steve Frith continues under the guidance of Adam Nicholas and Steve Merritt. This year we fielded a Rotary team of 23 to deliver a signature event that marks the start of our Rotary year.

- *Pictured from left Bill Boyes and Ernest Elbourne.*

THE ROTARY TOWN CLOCK

It is very difficult to capture the generational family commitment of the Proskowiec family in keeping the Town Clock functioning. George Proszkowiec of Terrace Showcase Jewellers and his family have been involved in re-designing the internals of the Rotary Clock and looking after it mechanically for about five decades.

The Rotary Clock, standing on the intersection of Port Stephens Street and William Street, Raymond Terrace was built by the Rotary Club of Raymond Terrace in 1955. The project was undertaken by the newly formed Club to commemorate the 50th anniversary of Rotary International.

During the 1954 and 1955 Rotary year the Club undertook fundraising activities to raise the funds needed (1500 pounds) to complete the project. However, the devastating 'big flood' of 1955 hit Raymond Terrace and the money raised was donated to the town flood relief. Not to be deterred, the following year the Club undertook further fundraising activities to complete the Clock Project.

From 1955 to 1970 maintenance of the Clock was carried out by well-known local, Fred Anseline who was a charter member of the Rotary Club. By the mid 70's with no one to maintain the Clock, it was handed over to the Port Stephens Council. However, the internal workings of the Clock needed attention. George's father, Wladyslaw Proszkowiec, was a member of the Rotary Club, and on his passing in 1974, his family, who were watch makers and jewellers in Raymond Terrace since 1967 decided, as a legacy and in memory of Wladyslaw, to undertake a complete modernisation of the clock working system.

George and his brother, Peter, had taken on quite a project and the Clock was restarted after the significant upgrade in October 1984.

Currently the Proszkowiec family are funding the costs and remain committed to the ongoing maintenance of the time keeping of the Clock as a service to both the community and to Rotary. George and Peter have the support of both their sons for the future.

This has been an amazing commitment by the family over so many years and the Rotary Club of Raymond Terrae are extremely grateful for their dedication.

Fortunately, the Council has maintained the external features of the clock and it is currently in the midst of a major refurbishment as the masonry and electricity supply are overhauled.

The Club acknowledges the efforts of George and Peter and their family together with the Port Stephens Council in keeping our landmark Clock a feature of Raymond Terrace.

Supporting Youth in our Community

Since being chartered in 1953, the Rotary Club of Raymond Terrace has forged strong connections with the youth of our area through schools, leadership initiatives and opportunities for young people. The Club has had a lifelong impact on many of our young people.

None better describes our passionate focus on youth than the Primary Schools Debating Competition, where each year up to 10 schools compete for monetary prizes and a perpetual shield, refining their public speaking and social skills under the guidance of their teachers.

The Club has been instrumental in funding student welfare and literacy programs at Irrawang and Grahamstown Public Schools. Our recent School Backpack Program saw hundreds of backpacks filled with stationery items donated to our local schools for distribution. An Interact Club, established at Irrawang High in recent years fostered leadership skills and knowledge of the world through service projects and activities.

Youth leadership programs have seen selected students from Irrawang High and Hunter River High attend Rotary Youth Programs of Enrichment (RYPEN) to build self-confidence, social skills, leadership skills and give them opportunities to become a better person. Young adults (18-25) have been sponsored to attend Rotary Youth Leadership Awards (RYLA), that gives them opportunities to enhance proven and potential leadership abilities. Numerous students have been sponsored by the Club for an International Youth Exchange for 12 months or a school Term to New Zealand. These opportunities have changed the lives of many young people, enabling them to learn another language, discover a different culture and become a global citizen.

The Club has provided opportunities for students to explore their passion for science and career opportunities in technology and engineering fields through sponsorship of Year 11 students from our District to attend the National Youth Science Forum at the Australian National University in Canberra for a weeklong conference in January. The Club regularly sponsors the Science and Engineering Challenge at Newcastle University.

The Club's focus in supporting leadership initiatives and opportunities for youth has always been an integral part of our program.

- *School Debating Competition 2023 Winner- Wirreanda Public School.*

FURNITURE BANK

In 2017 Past President John Chambers identified a need within the community for essential household items. At the time there were four separate women's refuges that were seeking assistance, and often when people were able to secure social housing, the house was empty. Donations are sought from the community as, in many cases, second-hand items are worth very little, but to those in need they can be like gold.

The Project is in keeping with our vision of 'giving a hand up', not a handout', as those we assist today generally come via a referral from other frontline agencies.' The following is the history of the Furniture Bank

- In 2017 the Furniture Bank quietly started out of a borrowed 20' container in the car park of an industrial shed complex in Heatherbrae.

- In April 2019 through the efforts of member Steve Frith the Club gained access to a 40' HI Cube container that Steve had accepted in exchange for plumbing work.

- In May 2019 the container was relocated to the property of past member Ken and Heather Buckingham.

- In 2019 / 2020 the Club purchased test and tag equipment to allow two members who hold test and tag authorities to test whitegoods that pass through the Furniture Bank.

- Throughout 2019 and well into 2021 the Club operated in association with the Salamander Bay Recycling Center that provided free of charge, items we required on an urgent basis to support those in need.

- In 2019 / 2020 the Club was successful in securing a Federal Government Grant to purchase a dedicated 8x5 single axle trailer with a 1000mm high crate and ramp to supplement the use of Club member trailers.

- In 2020 / 2021 the Club secured a Federal Government Grant to help in the purchase of two 40' HI Cube containers and the Council assisted us in securing Development Application approval to locate the containers on Council land in a disused car park.

- The Port Stephens Mayor in June 2021 also assisted by meeting the cost of the first year's site rental.

- In 2021 / 2022 the Club secured a Council Grant to refurbish our 15-year-old BBQ unit. This included replacing the trailer that carries the BBQ unit with a new 8x5 heavy duty trailer with crate and drop-down tailgate, so that when the trailer was not in use carrying the BBQ unit it could assist with the expanding Furniture Bank activity

- .In 2022 / 2023 the Furniture Bank secured a State Government Grant that will allow the expansion of the Furniture Bank to include a third HI Cube container. A "HI Cube" container, while more expensive, is 2700mm high instead of 2400mm maximizing the storage capacity of a container.

- Port Stephens Council assisted us to secure a variation to the Development Consent to allow a third container to be installed on the site.

- To assist members with the burden of vehicle running costs in the pickup and delivery of essential household items across the Port Stephens area, the Club reimburses the cost of fuel only that is funded through our various fundraising activities.

This year the Furniture Bank Program required members to undertake between 20,000 and 25,000 kms. With three to five deliveries every week and potentially nearly as many pickups the program has grown into a significant commitment for those involved.

- Pictured from left Adam Nicholas and Tara Ball from the Raymond Terrace Bowling Club.

Rotary with Pride of Workmanship Awards

- *Above: Some of our previous recipients.*

The Rotary Club of Raymond Terrace has supported many aspects of the community, from youth initiatives to networking organisations to presenting well attended community events to supporting major disasters encouraging strong leadership. The Business Community participates in these activities as well. Our Pride of Workmanship Awards affords them the opportunity to recognise staff who are key to their businesses.

Vocational Service has been a cornerstone of Rotary from the start recognising all occupations and contributing those talents to the problems and needs of the community. Always aspiring to high ethical standards, the motto used 'do it once, do it right'. Rotary's Pride of Workmanship Awards have led to other Awards recognising excellence and encouragement throughout the community.

Rotary members contact businesses and service providers in the months prior to the awards to establish a connection to these employers to not only support the awards but to also assist Rotary in its many leadership programs. Sometimes, the businesses are willing to provide the Club with a 'site visit' where the business is able to provide a snapshot of their processes and developments.

Recently the awards have expanded to include service industries as well as volunteer groups with Police, SES, Fire Brigade and Council work teams being among the recipients in the last few years.

Our upcoming Pride of Workmanship Awards will be held at the Raymond Terrace Bowling Club on October the 28th 2023. We are seeking nominations for the 2024 year. If your business has a person that you would like to have recognised through this award program, please do not hesitate to reach out to our President Adam Nicholas at pres.rotaryrt@gmail.com.

- *Pictured Recipients with Richard South.*

Afterword

Rotary makes a difference by serving to change lives

The Rotary Club of Raymond Terrace acknowledges the support it has received over the 70 years to provide a range of services to the Raymond Terrace community. Rotary members have continued to provide 'service above self' in order that the broader community can receive life changing benefits or to engage in community organised events.

Businesses and organisations have been generous to assist us in those programs with resources or funds which have complemented various grants received by the club to establish many programs that make a difference.

The community has also been supported in our many fundraising efforts at Christmas Raffles, Bunnings and other BBQs carried out initially in our heavy caravan to our much lighter BBQ trailer. You have also supported Australia Day, King Street Heritage Festival, Community Connect days and recently the 'Central' SES event.

Throughout the past 70 years there has been a desire, not only to give help where needed, but provide a platform to encourage leadership and development particularly in our Youth. All schools in the area have benefited with debates, programs of enrichment, leadership and the opportunity to expand their horizons with a yearly international exchange to all countries around the world, with the added benefit of inbound students giving us a better understanding of the world, as well as shorter exchanges with New Zealand. There have been literacy programs, donations and Backpack supplied to those doing it tough. Organising a driver training program with the police while short lived did provide a service utilising significant support in the community. The Furniture Bank again demonstrates an initiative that provides a hand up to those in need which has grown exponentially due to the requirements of the community but is again assisted by the generous donations from the public to ensure those needs are met in some way. There is a side benefit as some items might have ended up in land fill.

The Rotary family has expanded its outreach with new clubs established along the way with clubs at Nelson Bay, Williamtown/ Medowie and a second club in Raymond Terrace for a short time. Probus were formed in Raymond Terrace and Medowie.

National disasters and those overseas have not only received financial support, but members have travelled overseas to PNG and Africa to Rotary organised support programs. Worldwide contributions by Clubs with matching funding have assisted health programs to eradicate Polio and research for treatment of Malaria and other health issues. The club has provided several 'shelter boxes' to the pool of such boxes that are immediately despatched to countries of need. The boxes provide shelter and essential needs for 10 people.

Rotary Club of Raymond Terrace members are grateful for the opportunity to service the community and would welcome anyone with likeminded attributes to help us Make a Difference.

The Rotary 4 Way Test

Is a mirror in which to examine our own actions, words & integrity

Not a window through which to observe and judge other's actions

- Is it the TRUTH?
- Is it FAIR to all concerned?
- Will it build GOODWILL & BETTER FRIENDSHIPS?
- Will it be BENEFICIAL to all concerned?

www.ingramcontent.com/pod-product-compliance
Lightning Source LLC
Chambersburg PA
CBHW060428010526
44118CB00017B/2401